SAINTS ON THE STAGE

TILL THE GREEN WORD GREW

CATHERINE, MY MOTHER

BY

FR. DOMINIC ROVER, OP

INTRODUCTION BY
FR. MATTHEW POWELL, OP

2018

DNS PUBLICATIONS

Saints on the Stage
by Fr. Dominic Rover, OP

Introduction by Fr. Matthew Powell, OP

DNS PUBLICATIONS

Dominican Nuns of Summit

543 Springfield Avenue

Summit, New Jersey 07901

www.nunsopsummit.org

ISBN: 0999243241
ISBN-13: 978-0999243244

CONTENTS

INTRODUCTION

The two plays in this volume, *Till the Green Word Grew* and *Catherine, My Mother,* are the work of Father Dominic Rover, O.P. Born in Washington, D.C. in 1920, Thomas Rover left Georgetown University Law School to enter the Dominican Order where he received the religious name of Dominic. Shortly after ordination he was sent, along with Father Alan Morris, O.P., to the Yale University School of Drama to prepare for ministry at the Blackfriars Theater in New York City.

Blackfriars was an early Off Broadway theater founded in 1940 by Fathers Urban Nagle, O.P. and Thomas Carey, O.P. The New York Blackfriars grew out of the Blackfriars Guild, a Catholic theater movement begun in 1931 in Washington, D.C. by Father Nagle. By 1951 Father Carey, however, was alone at the New York Blackfriars and requested that the prior provincial assign two young friars for the theater ministry. After two years at Yale Fathers Rover and Morris joined the staff of Blackfriars. While at the theater the two young priests wrote four plays, all of which received favorable reviews from the New York drama critics. In 1957 Rover and Morris were assigned to other ministries. Rover went on to teach theology at the Dominican House of Studies in Washington, D.C. and at Providence College in Providence, Rhode Island. He also continued to write—poetry, scholarly works in theology, as well as television dramas. Friars who lived with Father Rover remember him as a man of great intelligence, charm and wit. In 1998 he died from Parkinson's Disease from which he had suffered for almost twenty years.

It was a young and healthy Rover, however, who in 1956, was asked by the producers of *The Catholic Hour* television program to write a series of scripts for them. Two of those plays are the ones contained here. *The Catholic Hour,* aired on both television and radio between 1953 and 1967, was produced by the National Council of Catholic Men and broadcast on N.B.C., the National Broadcast Company. The broadcasts offered a wide assortment of programming: lectures, music, documentaries and dramas. Topics covered included communism, racial equality, the role of the Church in government and ecumenism. Bishop Fulton Sheen was a popular presenter. Many Hollywood artists donated their talents. Rod Serling wrote some of its dramas and a young Martin Sheen was one of its actors. The program even broadcast an original short opera, *Dolcedo,* with script and lyrics by Rover and music by Emerson Myers.

Rover's writing of television scripts for *The Catholic Hour* was in line with Dominicans using every possible vehicle for preaching the Gospel. In the thirteenth century, for example, Blessed James of Voragine organized a troop of acrobats and jugglers from among the Dominican student brothers to mingle entertainment with his itinerant preaching. In the Province of Saint Joseph it had long been a tradition for the novices and student brothers to stage an annual play. Those plays were chiefly for the recreation and enjoyment of the brothers and the rest of the community. Rover's writing for *The Catholic Hour,* however, was a part of a broader use of theater as an apostolate carried on by the friars of the province that dates back more than 85 years. As was previously mentioned, Nagle founded the Blackfriars Guild in 1931 as a national Catholic theater movement. At its height the Guild had theater groups in twenty-two cities and a summer theater at Nabnasset, Massachusetts. The New York theater, founded in 1940 and located in the Broadway district, was its crown jewel. In addition to Rover and Morris other Dominicans penned plays for Blackfriars. Nagle wrote six plays, including the highly popular *City of Kings,* a dramatic biography of Saint Martin de Porres. Father Brendan Larnen, O.P. wrote seven plays, including *The Angelic Doctor* about Saint Thomas Aquinas. And Father Thomas McGlynn, O.P., primarily a sculptor, wrote the challenging and though provoking play, *Caukey.* In that drama Father McGlynn envisioned an America where racial roles are reversed, black people being the privileged elite and whites an oppressed and poor minority. Blackfriars operated until 1972 and gave starts to actors such as Geraldine Page, Patricia Neal, Eileen Heckart, Anthony Franciosa and Darren McGavin. More detailed information about Blackfriars is available in *God Off-Broadway: The Blackfriars Theater of New York* by Matthew Powell, O.P. (Scarecrow, 1998).

In 1937 Father Gilbert Hartke, O.P., a colleague of Nagle and Carey in the early Blackfriars movement, started the Drama Department at the Catholic University of America in Washington, D.C., a department he headed until his retirement in 1974. The CUA program eventually included graduate degrees, a summer theater and a national touring company. The CUA program produced actors such as Jon Voight, Philip Bosco and Susan Sarandon.

Also in 1937 Nagle and Carey became founding members of the National Catholic Theater Conference, an umbrella organization for Catholic parish, high school, college and independent drama groups. Carey was elected its first secretary. The organization's initial office was at the Catholic University of America, but in 1941 it was moved to the Blackfriars in New York. At its height the NCTC had 14,000 members, held an annual convention and published two periodicals. Rover wrote articles for *Drama Critique,* the group's scholarly journal. NCTC operated until 1970.

In 1970 the province's work in theater expanded further when Father Leo Pelkington, O.P., who had studied theater at the Catholic University, was assigned to Providence College to direct the Pyramid Players. Pyramid Players, the college's long established drama club, had always been directed by Dominicans, including in previous years Fathers Nagle, Larnen and Morris. In a few years Father Pelkington developed the extracurricular group into an academic program offering a B.A. degree in theater arts. Later Fathers Reginald Haller, O.P., Peter John Cameron, O.P. and Matthew Powell, O.P. (then of Saint Albert's Province) taught and directed in the department.

Finally, in 1998 Father Cameron re-founded the Blackfriars Guild as the Blackfriars Repertory Theater. Cameron had earned a master of fine arts degree in playwriting from the Catholic University of America and was an accomplished playwright. One of his well received plays is *The Sacrament of Memory,* based on the life of Saint Therese of Lisieux. The Blackfriars Repertory, located in New York City, has developed into a flourishing professional theater company, well respected by area audiences and drama critics alike.

Rover's television plays were forgotten after their original broadcasts and nearly lost. When Father Powell decided to produce *Till the Green Word Grew* for the 800th anniversary of the founding of the Order the only extant copy of the play was a yellowed typewritten manuscript. He produced *Till the Green Word Grew* in June, 2016 in Saint Dominic Chapel at Providence College as part of the province's celebration, the play's first production in sixty years. Later, after a long search, *Catherine, My Mother* was found.

While the two *Catholic Hour* plays in this volume were written for production on television, the dramas can be profitable spiritual reading. They can also be easily performed as staged readings, which eliminate the need for costumes and sets and allow women to impersonate the male characters and vice versa.

In addition the two plays are excellent examples of how the theater can be an effective tool of evangelization. Father Cameron's article, *The Role of Theater in the Evangelization of Culture* (available at blackfriarsrep.com/father-cameron) provides an excellent and in depth development of the topic of theater as evangelization. Also of note on the subject is a video presentation by Cameron given at the Faith and the Arts Forum in 2013 at DeSales University in Center Valley, Pennsylvania (also available at blackfriarsrep.com/father-cameron).

Till the Green Word Grew

A television play by Dominic Rover, O.P.

Originally produced on *The Catholic Hour* on N.B.C. Television
on April 1, 1956

CHARACTERS:

Raymond, Count of Toulouse

Dominic de Guzman

Bishop Diego

Enas, an innkeeper

Enas' wife

Godfrey, an Albigensian perfect

SCENE: An inn near Toulouse, France, about 1210.

Raymond:

(Coming forward and bowing)

Raymond, Count of Toulouse, your servant.

The world, as I speak, is old as time.

The Church—1200 years or more.

And Christendom a young giant.

The head strong but a fever on it

And a new shaking in the limbs.

We feel it here, too, in France.

You see, my kingdom has gone over

To the heresy, most of it, anyway—

The wealth, the large cities,

The nobility, and, of course, the

People follow.

Well, what was I to do|

Rome is so slow to move

And these lank prophets sprout

In the hills like sour weeds.

You know what they teach—

Life is evil, marriage ugliness

And shame, matter cursed—

Oh, a whole litany of curses

For all the pleasant toys

We play with. A hard doctrine

Yes, but man has a taste for gall,

For the text that wounds and kills.

Well, it's what they want.

They're proud of their thin-lipped saints

Walking the roads of Toulouse,

Bones picked clean with fasting,

Ready for the reliquary

Ten years before the grave.

Did you have something to say?

Dominic:

Dominic:

(To Raymond)

Forgive me. You speak so easily

Of a poison, as though we could leave

A field to weeds, rake it once

For conscience's sake, and then

Find rapture in the bloom,

Tangled as it is,

Tearing clothes, skin and eyes.

(To audience)

What did I know of it? Not much at first.

The fact is—I grew up, took orders,

Found my place in the Church

And scarcely heard of the Albigensian curse.

A few plague-spots in Spain, of course.

Not many.

Yes, I'm from Spain—Dominic of Guzman,

Canon, scholar, clerk to the Bishop

Of Osma, traveling now with his grace,

Though new to traveling, and to danger

And the acid taste of Manichean

Texts.

Yet once, my Lord, and here

In this very place, in your Toulouse,

I heard the nightmare cry of heresy

For the first time. I saw one soul

Caught and held like a plaintive bird

Cooling torn limbs with a wing

That used to fly. Here in his own

Inn where we rested.

I stood beside him-

Dumb I stood, awkward,

Mused and murmured there

Till God rose powerful and new

In me, tantalizing powers of speech

Till the green word grew

Out of my tongue-tied woe.

And zeal-of-the word for flower.

(Dominic and Diego warming themselves at the fire)

Diego:

A long day we had of it, Dominic,

A long journey. What do you think

Of the world now?

Dominic:

Greater than I knew in size;

No rest on the dusty roads.

Yet I think I could win a taste

For the world again, even after

Years of quiet. There's a longing

In the air cries out for priests.

Diego:

Yes. It's good to know that,

And to wonder why. But a sad day

When you begin to get used to it.

You're very tired tonight, young man.

Dominic:

Yes.

Diego:

Well, so am I. I warn you—

Don't cross me. There's no one

So testy as a hungry child

Or a Bishop fighting sleep.

(Enas, the Innkeeper, approaches with cups of wine.)

11

Enas:

Your wine, my Lords.

Diego:

Thank you.

Enas:

The meat is near to ready.

Will you have it here,

Or up in your room?

Diego:

Upstairs, if you please.

Enas:

Yes, my Lord.

(Stands, staring at them)

Diego:

Well?

Enas:

Is it Bishops you are?

Diego:

(with a smile)

One of us. The other works most patiently.

In the impatient shadow of a Bishop.

Enas:

Roman Bishops, is it?

Diego:

Diego of Osma, my canon—Dominic,

Sons of Spain and therefore of Rome.

Is there some other kind of Bishop?

Wife :

(At the fireplace)

Enas!

Enas:

Oh, yes, my Lord. We have our own here

In Toulouse, them walking by a law

Too hard for man. No meat,

Nor red wine, preaching no touch of woman,

They bearing a curse, every spawning one,

For the hope of life in the womb. A new kind,

All right, and a new Gospel, too.

Wife:

Enas!

Dominic:

A new Gospel?

Enas:

And not much hope in it

For a man with an inn, feeding the wicked

Body, keeping the flesh alive

When death is the only blessing.

Wife:

Enas!

Enas:

(To Dominic)

I know what's like, sire.

I have my own Bishop,

Called a wife. Pardon, my Lords.

(He crosses to his Wife.)

14

Dominic:

Did you hear him?

Diego:

Yes. They're everywhere, poor creatures,

With a devilish few to lead them

Called the Perfect. That's what

He meant by his Bishops

Dominic:

And our host, this man,

He's one of them?

Diego:

So it seems.

Dominic:

Here in this room.

Diego:

You're so surprised.

This is what you felt

Today and didn't know it.

Dominic:

Yes.

Diego:

Well, I'm warm enough and dry enough
And more than tired. Are you coming up?

Dominic:

Yes, my Lord.
(But he does not follow Diego.)

Dominic.

I'll be there soon.

Diego:

You have the eye of a hurt child
Who sees the forest-world of evil
For the first time.

Dominic:

It may be.
I'm struck to wonder
Like a child, like a man in love.

Diego:

You're choking for air, that's all,
A few days out of our quiet garden in Spain.

Dominic:

How can I know? To me
This seems like a new garden. I suppose
I'm too young to reckon what odd shape of bone,
Warp of tissue, evil takes when it nettles the brain,
Re-explores the heart. I don't pretend to know.
But a fountain moves in me, and I must
Watch it flow over this poor naked soul.

Diego:

You have a plan for persevering here?

Dominic:

Yes. To pray, to speak, then bold enough
To speak again, poor enough to pray.

Diego:

You think he'll listen to you?

Dominic:

I don't know. He may laugh, sleep,

Curse mightily, or even turn my tongue's fine

Edge to scorn. But he'll not say: "Where was

Christ when I walked blind in Albi." If God

Be with me, sir, I'll leave echoes here for ransom.

Diego:

Well, it's good to know you preach

To me first. Is it for practice or petition?

Dominic:

I'll need my Bishop's leave.

You see, if I'm sent,

I'll have no fear at all.

Diego:

Give a young man reason enough

To turn the world upside down

Or a young priest leave to set it right,

It's all the same. Not food, nor sleep,

Nor a moment's wasting. Well, go ahead.

Dominic:

Thank you, my Lord.

Diego:

Good night, Dominic. God be with you.

Dominic:

(Praying)

Be with me now. Be the ground

And motive of my longing,

And my clear way who may be wrong

To go forth and preach

When silence could be best,

A safe home for a foolish tongue

Like mine. What shall I do, Lord?

Shall I rest with thee

Or shake the bitter tree of heresy

Till little children fall?

Or if I have no choice

(for you have chosen me)

Where do I drive the stakes in him,

How deep, with what clean strokes

To make a little empty room

For the rush of thy love

Through the walls? God's blood

Wash, wash the heart of me.

Give me eyes to see,

Or eyelids dead

To scent the darkness of thy Will.

(Enas and his wife by the fire)

Wife:

You're an easy man

With your sweet courtesy to clerics.

Enas:

Guests of the house, mother. Guests.

Wife:

And what else?

Enas:

One a bishop. And a young priest.

Mother:

No place for them in a land

That's breathing pure again

Enas:

Just a meal and a bed, woman.

They'll be gone tomorrow.

Wife:

We should have locked the doors
And corked the wine up tight.

Enas:

Their money's good,
Not heathen money.

Wife:

It's worse. And you
Destined for the Perfect.

Enas:

That's not certain yet.

Wife:

They've spoken of you.
Godfrey talked in the square
Of the man from the inn
And his good helping wife.
There's talk of giving
The consolation to you.
Are you ready for it?

Enas:

Give me time, woman.

It's a hard life they're asking.

(During this conversation Raymond has drifted over near them.)

Raymond:

Yes, give him time.

Wife:

You're the Lord Count here,

Tell him, sire. The man's got a taste

For Christians and the Old Church.

Enas:

Caring for guests, is all,

Same as I give to everyone.

Wife:

And fighting the Consolation

If they want to give it to him.

Enas:

Not fighting, my Lord.

I'm not made for the hard ways.

                    Raymond:

No, you've some flesh to lose and a way

Of smiling. They'll trim you down, Enas,

That's sure.

                    Wife:

What of the strangers here?

                    Raymond:

Let them stay.

                    Wife:

You know who they are?

                    Raymond:

I know who comes and goes in my land.

Let them stay. We could use

Some entertainment for the night,

With your daughter locked upstairs,

And the wine come whining out

Like a miser, drop by drop,

Pleading an acquaintance.

With sums of water.

No, sir, it's good wine.

Good for thinning out a stew.

Is that one of our guests?

That's the young priest,

An honest young man,

Most grateful I ever seen

For a little courtesy.

Looks like a gulping fish

Heaved up on land for the first time,

Panting for prayers and curfews.

Shall we plague him, Enas?

Not here, sire. A good young man.

Yes, I know his kind.

Innocence on him like a bloom.

One word at variance

With constant, decet, lickety-licet,

He'll blush most maidenly from chin

To crown. Look. He wants you, Enas.

He wants someone. Give him a choice of wines, one

With fresh water, one with salt.

(Enas crosses to Dominic.)

Enas:

Did you call, sire?

Dominic:

Enas is your name?

Enas:

Yes.

Dominic:

A good name. And a good man, it seems.

But you opened up a mystery

To me and no answer yet.

You spoke of a new Gospel.

Enas:

It's what we've learned

From the Perfect. A poor man

Like me can't bear it all

In mind but I do my best.

Dominic:

What do they teach you?

        (Enas looks fearfully at his wife and at Raymond.)

No need to be afraid.

Enas:

It's about the gods—two of them.

The evil one's got hold of all

The lower things that make us like the beasts.

The other one's

All spirit, tugging at the flesh to

pluck us clean away.

Some'll fast and some'll die;

that way break clear. The rest of

Us....

        (He shrugs.)

We'll root around, maybe for all time,

Keeping flesh and wickedness alive.

Dominic:

Do you believe this?

Enas:

It's what they teach.
And living proof they are
With the hard and holy ways.

Dominic:

Does your wife believe this, too?

Enas:

Stronger than I do, sire.

Dominic:

And your children?

Enas:

We're bound to tell them,
Best we can and they understand.

Dominic:

Enas, listen to me, I know
The Gospels. Ten years I've prayed
And studied all the books

27

That tell of God and man

And the way to salvation.

None of this is true,

This is new preaching, none of it.

One God and that one good,

The body good in its measure,

And the soul, both together,

Making man, both good,

The earth good for feeding man,

The fruit of the tree blessed

And the fruit of the body.

Even now, as in the beginning,

God looks on all things save sin

And calls them good.

Enas:

Sounds fair and just, as you put it,

But it's not what the Perfect say.

Dominic:

Can you believe these are evil-

The glory of five fingers

On a stout arm, ease and power,

Bounty of the body, plus wife

And children, freshness of morning?

All evil? Enas. Answer me.

They're pleasant enough, that's true.

Oh, I tell you, sire, If I had

Some way to find life good, I'd

Want it so and not

All the pain and enduring

As they teach us now,

But, there's no turning back.

Dominic:

Theirs is a turning back

To a dark god before Christ.

Do you believe in our Savior?

Enas:

Yes, that he came preparing death . . .

Dominic:

To pass from death to life . . .

Enas:

Give suffering its place . . .

Dominic:

Yes, give it a place, not a throne,

Or a queen to rule with it—joy.

Is there no one left to teach

What's good and evil without invention,

No Church, no priests?

Enas:

They're gone, sir.

Dominic:

Gone?

Raymond:

Did you have a question, sire?

Dominic:

I was speaking to that good man.

Raymond:

If it's about the clergy, I can help.

Some few have passed into the ranks

Of the Perfect and not a memory of Rome

But turns to instant malediction.

Others, who find the role of Perfect

A damnable tight fit that splits

The seams of cassocks,

Have gone to seed. Weeds, sir,

A new breed of thistles.

Oh, we watch them bloom!

Dominic:

Who are you, my Lord.

Raymond:

A man who has a gift for turning.

Each head of an ugly little god

For mischief's sake, to mock the other.

I see it this way. Very simple. God is split in two,

The Earth is two, and man.

And so we have the same wild choice,

All of us—free to cultivate

A barren thirst

On the barren rocks as the Perfect do,

Our lie in tickling ease

In the cherry thicket yonder.

Dominic:

Choice? What choice

When there's a madness either way?

Raymond:

The one sane choice for each—

To be mad in one of two

Delightful ways. For me, of course,

One way. You see, I'm not fond

Of fasting, not yet.

I'm a different sort of jewel.

I shine to a darkened flaw.

No light gets through.

Dominic:

We all bring light of one sort,

Or darkness. We all preach.

Raymond:

You mean to Enas here?

Well, he's not my charge.

You chose him for your congregation.

Dominic:

I don't know. You act as though you very much

Cared what sweet soil or abominable dung of earth

These poor folk grew in.

Raymond:

Care? I honor them

By not caring, not snapping

At their heels like puppy dogs,

Shouting truth and falsehood for a fee.

Dominic

I'm sorry, my Lord.

We have a trick of barking.

We're hungry dogs

And awkward lovers.

Raymond:

It may be. But let's end all preaching

With one sensible word—pity

For the bleat and whimper

Of the five holy senses.

Dominic:

We're not cruel fathers

To every cry of the flesh.

Each is good in weight

And measure short of sin.

Raymond:

Sin? It's all sin, boy.

Dominic:

No. God's work is good.

Raymond:

Good? It's better than that.

Teasing evil it is.

That's the goblin truth

That kills and frees.

(A hermit-like creature enters, Godfrey,

One of the Perfect, dressed in tunic and cowl,

Long face, lean body, a voice out of a deep cellar of bones.)

Wife:

Your blessing, sire.

(She kneels and Enas does also, though more slowly.)

Godfrey:

Blessing in a house that breeds all

Manner of life that lingers?

Wife:

Please. A blessing on us.

Pitiful. Pitiful.

Godfrey:

(Extending his arms in a strange benediction)

When will the agony of life be done?

(He lowers his arm.)

Enas:

Yes, sire.

Godfrey:

Guests in thy house. I see them

How they lick at the wounds of pleasure.

Enas:

A poor man. It's a living

For myself and family.

Godfrey:

Know ye the Gospel truth?

35

Enas:

Oh, proper sire. Reading all
Times after working hours till
The eyes are dim. All the holy
Words.

Godfrey:

One word to remember.
Unless the seed die,
Unless it die . . .

Enas:

I know the rest. No fruit,
No fruit at all.

Godfrey:

(In a kind of chant)

To bear fruit is to die. Look
How the last greed of life
Clings to the earth,
To the hump-backed wood
On the fir, to the jealous eyes
Of men and beasts and the swollen fruit.
To bear fruit is to die.

Enas!

Enas:

Yes, sire.

Godfrey:

We ponder your life among the Perfect.

Will you come with us?

Enas:

Give me time, sire.

I've a wife to settle

And the tender children.

And there's others need my inn,

A good decent place, sire.

Godfrey:

Will you ask the Spirit to wait

Who moves over the water?

Enas:

(Shaking his head)

The Spirit knows I'm weak.

He'll let me think on it.

Godfrey:

No.

Enas:

Is there some other way, sire?

Godfrey:

Yes. There is another way.

Name the loves of earth

That bind you.

I'll bind them with a curse.

Enas:

No, sire. No curse.

Wife:

Not if it please you, my Lord.

He's a good man. He'll go.

Godfrey:

I'll bind them, strike them all—

To watch one soul go free.

Is it wine you love?

Enas:

Like any man.

Godfrey:

You'll find no pleasure in the cup.

The meal at midday?

(Enas nods.)

You'll choke on the day's bread,

Grow cold at the fire

That used to warm you,

Your wife a stranger,

Children all distaste, memory

Of the power of beasts that got them.

Then—then, you'll come

To the days of grief and fasting,

And not an eye to cast behind

Where all loves lie like stones.

Enas!

Wife:

Go with them before the curse,

Before it falls on all of us that's left.

Enas:

Give a man one night to muddle

The question. One night.

Godfrey:

No . . . no.

Wife:

Tell him you'll go, man. Tell him.

Godfrey :

(Raising his arms)

Maledictio spiritus maligni

Dominic:

What right have you to curse?

(Godfrey stops.)

No right!

(Godfrey lowers his arms.)

Can man claim

Power over God's world

To call it evil, or make it so?

Godfrey:

Even where the Spirit reigns,

A voice calls out—to resist

The Spirit. Who is this?

Wife:

A stranger, sire.

We hardly know him.

He's not to be listened to.

Raymond:

Leave them alone, mother.

Let them play the Gospel-game.

Can't you see? They're dicing

For that wooly grumbling prize

You call a husband.

Godfrey:

A stranger?

Dominic:

No.

A priest of our Holy Church

Who'll not let curses fall

So easily where he stands.

I am that priest. Who are you?

Godfrey:

Godfrey, once a sinner,

Now fit to call down judgment

Where Sodom reigns—or Rome!

Raymond:

Good, it's spoken.

They're matched and waiting.

Shall I clap or shout

Or ring a candle-bell

To start the disputation?

Dominic:

Please, my Lord. There's grave work

To be done for a poor man,

Peace to be given in Christ's name.

Godfrey:

What peace

When the nagging flesh brags, runs whining to Rome for judgement.

I know your kind of peace.

Will you hold him here with honey,

You who claim to preach the Cross?

Dominic:

I'll hold him with a promise

That the Cross brings life,

And honey in its own season.

I claim him with a promise.

Will you claim him with a curse?

It's your soul, Enas,

Yours to judge. What beauty

Is there in his one mad will

To deny the beauty of the universe?

Godfrey:

Blind beauty of the mind,

With the spirit free,

And the flesh bitten with a curse.

You forget.

I have power to free

This man with one word.

Dominic:

Then set him free, if you can.

Call it a curse or whatever you will.

Enas:

No, sire, don't tell him that.

I know him. He's a man

Loves the work of cursing.

Dominic:

No! Let his maledictions leap

Into the sun of this night

And fall back shocked with darkness

Till he damn every living thing in

This room.

Enas:

No. No, sire!

Dominic:

Trust me, Enas. It's the only way.

(Then, to Godfrey)

Are you afraid? Every eye

Is open. We're all nerves

And heart-beats, waiting.

We'll be quick to catch

The scent of evil

Like a sweet powder on the fire.

If there's God or devil

In your curse, we'll know it,

Or if there's nothing!

Godfrey:

(After a pause, raises his arms)

Maledicitio spiritus maligni

Descendat super vos

Et omnes creaturas cerperales.

(There is a long moment of silence as Enas and his wife kneel,

Trembling under the impact of the curse.)

Dominic:

Get up, Enas.

(Enas looks at him but cannot move.

Dominic extends an arm to help him rise.)

Put one living hand on another.

We'll both stand and test the earth.

Get up.

(Enas rises, slowly and awkwardly.)

Look about you.

It's the same winning world.

(He points to the jug.)

Did he curse the wine?

No. Drink it. Enas.

(He hands him a cup. Enas looks at it, hesitates, tastes it.)

And the bread, all pocked

And blushing from the fire.

(To Enas' wife)

Your good bread, mother.

No curse, no flaw.

(pointing to the fire)

Look! Did one mongrel coal

Leap up at his word,

Leap to a four-footed rage,

Or all sleep as now,

A blessed warmth, where you laid

The fire this early evening?

Enas, stretch your old loves' hands

To the four walls of this inn,

Your world, your little tent

Under the Lord's great tent,

Where his gifts bring an hour

Of peace or a long quiet night of it

(Enas looks around, seeing the room as though for the first

Time. His face takes on not a smile but a sign of peace.)

I, who have virtue from the placing

Of hands, I tell you power is given

From above for one cause, to lift

All curses with the Blood of Christ,

Or the promise of His Blood.

(Then, to Godfrey)

In the name of that sweet name

Leave this man alone.

He'd look so poorly

In the rags of the flesh you wear.

His children wouldn't know him.

Godfrey:

Let him speak for himself.

He knows what wound grows

On the body of man,

To be cut, to be burned.

Dominic:

Yes, he knows, if God be true

And Mary his for mercy

And for mother. Let him speak.

Enas:

This is my house, and my friends.

What walls I built

For holding a little warmth

Against the night, I'll not see

Struck down with curses,

Nor the good wine spoiled.

If you're not come to join us

In a cup, you may leave, sire.

You're not to come

To my house again.

Godfrey:

(In a final malediction)

There's a man here who's bent on souls.

Go with him, Enas,

And you catch contagious life!

(He exits.)

Raymond:

Might I ask a question?

Who won? Oh, Enas, you're a sly one.

You did. You get your curse

From one archangel

Whose specialty is curses

And your blessing from another

Who claims power to bless.

Dominic:

And you, my Lord, what have you to offer

To the good man, our host?

Raymond:

I? One word. Be what you are.

A man. Who can yawn away

A curse or a blessing

Or a scolding wife.

And my word to you? Leave him alone.

He'll be miserable and gay,

Drunk and sober by turn,

Up all day with a dream

Of love and work, bedded down

At night like a snoring beast.

Leave him alone. He'll grow tired of life

in his own good time.

Enas:

I'm not tired yet, my Lord,

And willing to find a few reasons

For a puzzle of life.

If it's too ugly to be borne,

This man will tell me why.

If too sweet, I'll learn

What new taste I need

To savor it. I've a slow head

For heavy thoughts but it seems just

What he says about God and the world

And I'll hear it out

If it takes the night.

I'll ask you watch the fire, mother,

While I talk to the man of God.

Raymond:

(Moving forward into the camera)

And so they went, to speak or pray

Or whistle pious hymns

Through the holes in their teeth

For all I know or care.

Fools will still make vigil

For a cause they love,

Still tremble success

Or failure in a matter

I call a bother and a bore.

He spoke to me later, the young priest.

He was gay as morning then-

Enas stood by him

His catechism fresh in mind new

And gratitude the final text.

Then he spoke to me.

(He laughs.)

We traded sermon for sermon.

"Take your talent for preaching,"

I said, "to a holier place.

When you speak in an inn

The word is like a head of ale,

Or should be—light and thick

And easily blown away."

He took my advice, the young fool,

Talked to the Pope, plucked

Young dreamers from the best families

And made preachers of them like himself.

Worse! They came trooping back to my country

And a dozen more.

Sons and Brothers of a new Order

Called Preachers after Dominic.

Monks by night, troubadours by day,

Piping to souls on street corners,

Setting the old dead words

To a dancing tune . . .

(His gentle cynicism turning into sadness)

. . . for those

Still young enough to dance.

I'm not. I'm tired of all

This quibbling over what's true and false. I'm tired of it.

What does it take to make

A man care about these things—

About God and his own soul

51

And a sure way to heaven?

What does it take?

Is there no word left for me-

A word strong enough to rule a people,

Gay enough to do the work of wine,

Sad enough to breed upon

When a man feels sad;

To give him rest, yet passion of sort.

Is there no one cheating chord

To strike when pleasure dies?

Dominic, and all your sons, is there no

Word left for me?

Dominic:

(In habit)

For you and all men—one word

Which was in the beginning

And ever shall be,

Who spoke once in time

our sweet Savior

Making the prophets true

Whose word I now take abroad

For a sword and a friend

Daring the length of it the time's end

Till I win, and blessed with God's booty

Scatter pennies of light to the poor.

THE END

Catherine, My Mother

A Television Play by Dominic Rover, O.P.

Originally produced on *The Catholic Hour* on N.B.C. Television on

January 14, 1962

CHARACTERS:

Catherine Benincasa

Lapa Benincasa, her mother

Raymond of Capua

Fra Lazzarino

Pope Gregory XI

Francesco Malavolti

The set is very simple and spare. Perhaps a series of ramps raking down toward a low center where a large cross is set. Before the cross Catherine of Siena is kneeling, rapt in prayer. Her eyes are closed, her arms are crossed in

front of her, but extended a little from the body with the palms out. Around her, and placed rather formally in the beginning, are five figures—her mother; her confessor, Raymond of Capua; Fra Lazzarino, the Franciscan theologian; Pope Gregory XI and Francesco Malavolti, a Sienese nobleman and bon vivant. We catch them in a kind of tableau at the start, though after the camera moves in on her mother, they should move out of range and enter only as we need them. In other words, the placing of the characters is very arbitrary and presentational. During the opening voice—over camera should remain fixed on Catherine, but on Catherine as the center of the group. We should feel their relation to her very strongly, but we should see chiefly Catherine in ecstasy.

VOICE:

Her name was Catherine Benincasa, known to us as Catherine of Siena. In the history of the inner life, Catherine was unique, so powerfully did God's Kingdom prosper in her, so wonderfully did it extend itself to the world around her—to Popes and princes, monks and priests, playboys and pious women, to all who were called "The Caterinati," that is formed by Catherine, mothered by Catherine, made like to her and to this holy Kingdom within her. The first also to be repelled by it were the members of her own family, and especially her mother.

Lapa separates herself from the group and moves into the camera. Opening credits and announcements are heard and seen as the group around Catherine disperses in a slow formal movement and as Lapa takes up a central position for her opening lines.

Lapa:

I am Lapa. Papa Benincasa, my husband, is a dyer named Giacomo. And this—this is my daughter, Catherine Benincasa, the holy one of Siena. For myself I don't like that kind of talk but let it be, I can't help what they call her. My youngest one she was, my baby. She came into the world with a twin sister, Giovanna, who died soon after and, I've said more than once, "I wish she had died too, I wish they had both died!" God forgive me! But I nursed her myself, this little one, because she was the last, and she grew up stronger than any of my girls. It's a fact. No, she wasn't pretty like Bonaventura, but she could have been. She was strong and straight and when she sat in the sun with her sister her hair began to turn light and bronzed, the way the young men liked it then. But no, she had that room upstairs, and the long prayers at night, even as a child, and when she sat at table she'd drop her meat to the cats under her feet and eat only bread and herbs, and then smile like an angel and tell me not to curse when I scolded her. I told Giacomo, I told her—it's not good to live this way, to turn away from the world, and men, and the beauty of your own body when you're young and strong with the power in you of a wife and mother! God is hard

57

sometimes. He's hard! Why does He take our babies away from us when they're too young to know what the world is and too young to die to the world, even for Him! God forgive me!

She blesses herself quickly.

But he wanted my baby almost as soon as they took her out of my body. He wanted her from the beginning. And then as she grew, and the prayer grew inside her, and people began to know what she was, and the crowds gathered around her—I hated them, I hated them all! The Mantellate with their pious faces and the young priests gaping at her, calling her 'Mama,' plus a few renegades to give the people something to talk about. Is this what you want for her, God? Is this what you've done to her? Who does she belong to? To her own family? To her own mother? To her husband and children who will never be? No, she belongs to them, to them, to that pack of dogs and owls and scrawny cats. She belongs to You or to them but never to me! Why did you bother to call her by my name and Giacomo's when she belongs only to You and to that pestilent mob she calls her children?

She crosses herself again, in a sudden fear.

No, no, I'm sorry, Jesus. I'm sorry. You take her, take her. I am an old woman and I have many children. Take her. How can I say that? How can I give You what belonged to You from the beginning, what belonged to You before I heard my first baby cry in the small bed under the big one where I could reach my hand down at night and coax my babies back to sleep...yes, yes, she belongs to You, Jesus...Catherine, my baby, who belongs to God.

She drops to her knees beside the kneeling figure of Catherine, leans against her gently, her emotions spent. The figure of Raymond of Capua comes out of the shadows, approaches the two kneeling women, lifts Lapa to her feet, takes her to a small stool, sits her down. She remains there, head down, hands in lap.

Raymond:

I am Raymond, of the family of delle Vigne of Capua, by the grace of God a Christian, a priest and a member of the Order of Friars Preachers, appointed by the Master of my Order to be confessor and guide to this woman, this holy virgin whom I am pleased to call my penitent, my friend, my child and—yes, I will say it—my mother in Christ. I know her in all these ways and yet how can I describe her to you, and what the Lord Jesus has done in her? Her soul is bathed and immersed and buried in God. She is like one who dives into the sea and swims under the water for endless hours, neither seeing through the water the things that are outside the water, but not otherwise. Yes, she is like a fish, God's holy fish who lives only in water and the water is God. For my own part I confess I learned more by listening to her for ten minutes than she ever learned from me in a score of conferences. What she knew was from God and the way she knew it was from God; it ran pure and true like water from a fresh spring in the hills. I might as well confess this too, that I had my doubts about her, many times. I remember once in the convent in Montepulciano. She was sick with a great fever on her, she wanted to talk; so many things had happened to her—new visions, heavenly favors so great she could scarcely find tongue to tell of them. Then the flood of words about God's Blood and the Bridegroom and the need for a holy hatred of self, so strong this time that it stung me. It was, perhaps, the fear and guilt in my own soul, or else the devil himself got into my heart, but I began to wonder whether it was truly the Spirit of God who moved her or only the fever, and whether some mad fever of the soul had not always possessed her, from the beginning. What was it—fear, resentment, a trick of the devil? All those things, no doubt, and all at once. She lay there in front of me, flushed and babbling (so I thought) and it struck me that these holy words were all lies, lies of a wretched woman possessed of demons, or simply mad! Then I looked again at the virgin and suddenly it was not Catherine! It was the face of — the face of a man —looking up at me, with strong eyes and a short fair beard. Majestic—like the Byzantine Christ in the church of Monreale. It was terror held me there, a great terror, but I had to speak. "Who art thou?

Who?" And the voice answered: "He who is." At that very moment the face vanished and it was Catherine who lay there, cooled of her fever now, sleeping like a babe, or caught up in prayer which for her was like a long sleep and the end of pain. I stood by her,

He looks tenderly at the kneeling figure.

looking at the grave sweet face, as I look at her now. And my heart grieves that I should ever have doubted the true bride of my Lord Jesus Christ.

For a brief moment he kneels on one knee beside Catherine in front of the crucifix, then he goes over to Lapa, puts his hands on her head in a fatherly gesture and freezes there. As he does, a brown-robed Franciscan is seen approaching. It is Fra Lazzarino. He looks tenderly at Catherine and then at us.

Fra Lazzarino:

I am Fra Lazzarino, former lecturer in theology at the Franciscan convent in Siena and, so my friends say, the finest preacher north of Florence. It was Catherine here who formed the topic of many of my sermons in those days when I drew such crowds to the church of San Francesco. I knew her—by hearsay, by idle talk, by fantastic rumor; all of which to me spelled out self-deception, heresy even, plus a wayward desire to bind souls to herself like children who are bewitched! But I was a learned man and did not wish to live by rumors and idle talk. No, I had to see for myself and catch her in the very trap she was setting for others. I went to my 'friend,' the Dominican teacher Fra Bartolomeo, who had so rashly supported the virgin. I went to him and asked him to arrange a meeting. He took me to her cell. She greeted me with great sweetness and reverence and then sat at my feet. It was scripture I thought to catch her on (she had made some wild explanation of Christ's agony in Gethsemane) but when I asked for enlightenment, she turned to me for guidance, speaking of my learning, my many degrees, my reputation as a teacher of Divine Truth. When I left, she asked for my blessing like any pious woman, and like any pious friar I asked her to pray for me. Quite commonplace the entire meeting and in view of my heavy work schedule almost a waste of time. I returned home and went to bed. When I awoke the next morning, my soul was like lead! I had an important lecture to give that very morning but I could not move. Some unutterable grief weighed down on me and as I tried to think and to write I began—unthinkably for me—I began to weep! I leaned like a heart-broken child against the wall of my cell and wept, and wept.

He breaks a little now, thinking about it.

And I did not know why! There were no answers, no reasons, but the burden of grief remained. I called off the lecture and lay there all day in my room, groaning on my bed like a rejected lover, unable to work, unable to think. Dusk came. I lighted the lamp on my table determined to draw up an outline for tomorrow's lecture. I looked at my room—the papers, the books, the crucifix, the little woodcarvings I made as my one diversion. I looked at my room but I could see in my mind's eye another room where the lamp burned before another crucifix and a frail young woman sat at my feet with her bright eyes looking into mine, her face pale like a flower I had soiled merely by looking at it. Yes, yes, it was at this very moment the day before that I had been with her! And then, as in the morning, though now like the breaking of dammed water over rocks, I wept unbearably! How long? I do not know. But when it ceased, I did the one thing I could do to ease the pain; I went to see her and knelt at her feet. She tried to make me rise. No, I knelt there, asking for mercy, asking her to teach me what it was like to be a follower of Christ. If she had not been there to console me, I think I would have gone mad thinking of the empty words of a hundred thunderous sermons, my voice turning glorious colors like autumn leaves to echo the simple truths of the Gospel. Jesus, forgive me! Catherine warned me not to think of these things too much, so bitter it was to remember, but it does not matter now. When a man is truly free, he is free also to remember. I gave up my lecturer's chair, my pulpit, my precious books—save for a few I kept to mediate on. With my guardian's permission and that of the Minister General of the Order I made plans to live in a hermitage. It was some months before I could go and I learned then how our Savior purifies a soul He has saved from its own folly. Little children were pushed out of the doorways by their parents to mock the great preacher who had mocked at Catherine. And my own brethren! Well, I had better not speak of this; they had reason enough to taunt me. And, after all, these were precious days and nights when the Lord Jesus let the words of others be the whip and spittle and bitter wine of my own blessed Passion. For I say before God there is no happiness like this, to be one with Him in sorrow, and one with her, for this child is my mother in Christ.

He falls on his knees by Catherine facing the cross and is lost in a deep and humble prayer. Suddenly Raymond stirs, sensing the approach of someone he looks and we look with him and see a white clad figure in pontificals entering. Raymond rouses Lapa, then moves to make Fra Lazzarino aware of the approach of Gregory XI.

Raymond:

I beg you be quiet and most reverent in your demeanor. His Holiness, Gregory XI, is approaching.

Raymond then turns and kneels as does Lapa and Fra Lazzarrino. The Holy Father walks through them, benevolently, bestowing his blessing. He goes to Catherine, looks down at her tenderly. A flicker of emotion on his face, then a blessing for Catherine.

64

Raymond:

No doubt, his holiness will speak to you. For he too is a friend of Catherine Benincasa.

Gregory speaks with great dignity, but with a weariness on him, the weariness of a man with great public burdens and an honest sense of his own limitations. There is something touchingly equivocal in his reaction to Catherine. He is immensely grateful for her help, believes thoroughly in her divine inspiration, yet he cannot let go of the idea that she has pushed him to act beyond his strength and beyond the human prudence he is still inclined to rely on. He loves her and fears her and sometimes wishes he had never met her.

Gregory:

Yes, I know the virgin of Siena. I know her as I knew the holy seer Bridget of Sweden, who was also my friend and counselor. Indeed the jest going round the Papal Court at Avignon is that my reign thus far has been the reign of one man besieged by two women. Two women, both of God with voices like archangels and pens like running fire, for they can write letters as long as the tracts of Origen, so that I spend all day reading them and all night fretting over an answer. Bold letters biding me launch a new Crusade, at once! Pleading letters that I might forgive the Florentines after a fresh revolt. Scolding letters urging me back to Rome, back from Avignon to a Rome more corrupt than the court they find such a scandal here in France. When Bridget died—God rest that soul!—Catherine took up the task alone, as though in a moment the Spirit of God had sped from Sweden to Siena with a flaming sword and sheathed it in the fiery fist of Catherine! And yet I could not tell you, I could not possibly describe it; she is soft and fair as any woman, as no woman who ever lived since the Virgin her Queen. Under the iron words there is a heat so gentle, so loving, that I kneel at my *prie-dieu* and think, "It is well with the Pope; it is well with Gregory; it is well with the man born Pierre Roger Beaufort" because Catherine is with him and Catherine is for him." I am not ashamed to say this to you, that I, the Holy Father, listen to her saying to me, *babbo mio dolce*, 'my sweet father,' and at that moment I do not know what else she could call me. As for my Counselors, especially those of my own family, she calls them 'devils,' some of them 'incarnate devils.' I don't know. It seems too strong to me. Yet sometimes—behind a smile or a frown—I see what she sees and the whole of Christendom seems set upon by smiling, frowning devils! while the Body of Christ bleeds at Rome and Florence and Avignon with the wounds of a thousand years! . . . and so at last I am back in Rome, as she wished. The 'Mama' has placed her 'sweet babbo' back in the old bedeviled crib. Some days are all glory and freedom as I look out on the streets of Rome after a fresh rain and know it is well for me to be here. I am strong and ready for fresh crosses. And the next day I awake with clamoring fears and say Mass with all the cares of Christendom flickering in the candles. No one, no one knows the enemies I have here in Rome! I spoke of death when I came here and death is still the gift Rome wants dearly to give to her French Pope. And not even Catherine can stay the hands of all the devils who itch to see me fall! I am a man of peace and when she is not with me, when I do not hear from her for a month, when her voice is not singing bravely in my ear, I am afraid.

He covers his face with his hands, as though blotting out the fearful images of violence and death. He recovers slowly and deliberately, composes himself, invests himself again with the power and gravity of Peter.

Gregory:

That is why I ask you to pray for me, all of you. To pray for Gregory; to pray for Peter that his faith fail not, so that being strengthened he may bring strength to all his brethren in Christ.

He turns and takes his place kneeling in front of the cross with Catherine. A mocking laugh is heard and we pick up the young nobleman Malavolti approaching the group kneeling around Catherine.

Francesco:

You see? You see, it is true. She has not lost one scrap of her power, even in the sleep of prayer. I always said she was the most powerful woman in Italy, in the world! Oh, I am the one they call Malavolti, Francesco di Messer Vanni Malavolti, son and heir of one of the great houses of Siena. I met the virgin Catherine through my friend Neri, the most pleasant of all companions, though not as rich as I, not as dissolute. On a dare he took me to see her (she was the one girl in Siena I had never spoken to) and I went, vowed to conquer her or curse her, but never listen to her holy preaching. I confess I found her fair but as I looked at that lovely face—never had this happened to me before—my eyes broke, my tongue failed me, and I began to tremble like a schoolboy. All the vile and brutish happenings of my life rose up in my mind like images of beasts, and suddenly the beasts were free and gone, and I felt a new heart in me like the heart of a young boy who has never once roamed like a faun in the fields round Siena. How could it be? I, Malavolti, the most eligible satyr in Siena! Night after night I sat at her feet listening to those pure and radiant words. I followed her to church with the rest, with those pious fools I had laughed at. Impossible!

Then, more sadly

Yes, it was. Impossible. One night I stayed away and went roaming with my friends, not Neri but the others, a fine band of brigands and lechers! I fell once more, in my usual trysting-place, the young faun browsing again on the old bitter herbs and roots. That's the way it was, no excuses. But the next evening like an obstinate fool I went with the rest to see Catherine. She looked at me, with those eyes of a mother, with the eyes of a wounded angel, and immediately bade the others go. "Francesco, my wild bird, come here. When were you at confession last?" "On Saturday," I said, and it was true, I had been. "When will you go again?" "On Saturday next, madre, as you have taught me." "You will go at once!" "Dearest madre, I will go tomorrow, which is Saturday. There will be time." Then the flame in her struck and lit up the pale face like the red veins in a flower. "Do you think I do not know what you have done? Do not my eyes and heart follow my children wherever they go? At this time and this place, you met." I clapped my hands over my ears so as not to hear the words I knew better than she. No, not better, for she knew everything, and knows everything now.

He looks at the kneeling figure, almost consoled at knowing that she knows, but bitter because he cannot respond to her understanding and love. He speaks to us.

Francesco:

Do you know what it is to go back to her, so many times, and to slip away, again and again! All of her friends, the Mantellate, everyone, told her: "Let him go, he is worthless, he is lost." And always she took me back. Always she smiled at her friends and took me back. "He is a wild bird, my Francesco," she would say, "but he shall not escape my hands. Just when he thinks I am far away, I will throw a noose round his neck and one day he will be caught for good."

He shakes his head sadly.

No, that day will never come. She will throw out her net and gather in all living things from sea and earth and sky. But the wild bird Francesco is free, not to be tamed, not to be caught, not to be plundered and felled by love!

He looks at her lovingly, then walks slowly away from her, as down a long corridor.

Goodbye, dolcissima mama. Goodbye. Out of so many you have lost one son. I will not torment you. I will leave you at peace. Goodbye.

As Francesco walks away, Catherine opens her eyes and becomes instantly aware of everything. There is no confusion in her, no sense of a distracted or detached state of mind. A moment ago she was deep in prayer: now she is the awakened mother, very much alert, terribly aware of the needs of her children, of each of them. Nor is she at all languid or ethereal in her personality. She is a woman—strong, alive, practical, loving, with an astounding dignity and power of command.

Catherine:

Francesco, Francesco.

Raymond moves to intercept the fleeing Francesco.

Catherine:

No, leave him alone. He must come on his own or not at all.

She rises and watches him go.

Catherine:

He will come back; my wild bird will come back. Not now, not in my lifetime, but in God's time, because I am his mother and he is my child.

She turns to the Pope.

Catherine:

My sweet Father in Christ,

She kneels for his blessing. He gives it, then draws her to her feet.

Catherine:

Babbo mio, you are sad. Why?

He is suddenly shy and silent, a little afraid—as always—to face her and her powerful instinct for the truth.

Catherine:

Is it for the same reason?

He nods assent.

Catherine:

You wish to leave Rome again.

Gregory rouses himself and becomes suddenly strong and aggressive.

Gregory:

It is different now, little mother! Word has come, through friends, that there is a plot on my life. The Florentines again. I know, I know what you are thinking: "He has grown soft and fearful. It is back to Avignon and new exile," but that is not the point. There is danger; the danger is in Rome; and here I am—in Rome!—exposed right and left to God knows what! And for what purpose?

Catherine:

For the purpose of keeping Peter in the city of Peter! For the purpose of staunching and binding the wounds your exile has caused in the Body of Christ.

Gregory:

No, no, little Mother, this is too simple.

Catherine:

Is it death you fear? But babbo mio, if it comes you will die in Christ's Blood for it is His Holy Will that you be here. If you do not die, then you were a fool to be anxious about it. This is simple. Yes.

Gregory: *exasperated*

What can I do to convince you?

Catherine:

You cannot convince me. You know that.

Gregory:

Then why did I come to speak to you about it?

Catherine: *deliberate and strong*

Because you know in your heart I am right. And you want me to support you with God's truth. Even against yourself. Is it not so?

Pause

Gregory:

Yes, you know me very well, little mother.

Catherine:

And you know me—that I will never give in.

Gregory:

Yes.

Catherine:

With tenderness but with a great sense of authority

So, it is all over, babbo mio. It is, indeed, very simple.

75

Then, smiling

If you could see your face now. You are beginning to be strong and free again. Oh, it is good not only to be a Pope but look like a Pope.

She kneels and he blesses her. She rises.

Catherine:

Now, go! Rome is your mother and your daughter and your sweet bride.

Gregory turns and walks away, slowly, solemnly. As Gregory moves away, Fra Lazzarino moves toward her, falls at her feet. He seizes one of her hands and kisses it passionately.

Catherine:

No, no, sweet Father. They will say you are one of Catherine's fools and as mad as she.

Fra Lazzarino

It does not matter what they say. You have brought me such happiness.

Catherine:

Then do what you will. This is the mark and sign of God's children—that they are happy in possessing His love.

He kisses her hand again.

Catherine:

In your heart kiss the hand of Jesus who has given us everything. How tender God makes the souls of men when they know they are loved!

He rises and moves away, in great peace.

Goodbye, babbo mio. Remain always in God's peace!

She turns to the others.

You have come too, Brother Raymond.

Raymond:

Yes.

Catherine:

I wondered if I would see you again. You have been so busy.

Raymond:

I have the kind of easy name the Pope and Bishops think of instantly when there is unpleasant work to be done for the Church.

Catherine:

That is the most exquisite suffering of all. Does it hurt, little Father?

Raymond:

It hurts.

Catherine:

Good. No one will know you are made holy by it.

Raymond: *(more urgently)*

But that is why I want to see you. I think of these missions and busy affairs and the traveling, and then I think of you. I think of your premonition the last time we met.

Catherine:

That we would not meet again.

Raymond:

Yes.

Catherine:

Perhaps this time it is really true.

Raymond:

That is why I must speak to the Holy Father and be relieved of this work.

Catherine:

No.

Raymond:

When I leave you, little mother. I am not the same. I am filled with cares and fears; I become so great and important.

Catherine:

That is the warfare for you, babbo mio. I have told you that. That is the wound you hold up for healing.

Raymond:

I want to stay with you! I want to stay!

Catherine:

Yes, and I want you to be here. But it is not the way now. You belong to God and to the Church, and Christ's Blood now washes us apart, like a river that divides two cities. It is so!

She sees his sadness.

We will always be together in Him. I in you and you in me, yet I know also in Jesus that we will never meet again.

He kneels suddenly at her feet. She is less tender than strong, knowing the need of firmness, sure of the source of his strength and hers alike.

Catherine:

Go, little Father! Go, in God's Blood!

She is straight and strong as he moves away. Then she turns and goes over to Lapa, puts her hands on Lapa's shoulders. Her mother seizes one hand and kisses it possessively, holds on to it.

Catherine:

Mamma, little mamma.

Lapa clutches her hand, but will not look at her.

Catherine:

Do not be ashamed before me of how you have felt. I could not always tell you what Our Lord Jesus was doing to my soul.

Lapa:

I am pleased. I am blessed at what He has done for you, but what is to become of me, with your Father dead and you belonging to everyone?

Catherine:

You will go with Bonaventura. What does she have now, seven children?

Lapa:

Yes, seven.

Catherine:

And do they not need a grandmother?

Lapa:

Who knows?

Catherine:

You can give them so much, Mamma mia. Such a wonderful cook and you always knew the secrets in the hearts of children. What is it, Mamma? There is something else.

Lapa nods almost in tears.

Catherine:

What is it?

Lapa:

I am not forgiven.

Catherine:

That is not true!

Lapa:

I held you back. Like a poisoned vine. All my life I held you back from God!

Catherine:

But that is all over, mamma mia. It does not matter. You give me to Him now, you do not hold me. Is that true?

Lapa nods.

Catherine:

Then all is forgotten.

She embraces her mother.

I belong to you now much, much more than if He had never taken me. Do you believe that?

Lapa nods assent.

Catherine:

This is the way with God's love. What He has given He takes, because He is God. But what He takes He gives back, so that in the end everything is twice-given and everything belongs to Him. Do not cry, my baby, my baby.

Catherine comforts her as the first and last of her children, rocking her back and forth like a baby in her mother's arms.

THE END

www.ingramcontent.com/pod-product-compliance
Lightning Source LLC
Chambersburg PA
CBHW060529030426
42337CB00021B/4192